GW00888598

RECIPES

by Carole Gregory

with illustrations by A.R. Quinton

ANNE HATHAWAY'S COTTAGE, SHOTTERY

J. SALMON LTD., SEVENOAKS, KENT

*I*NDEX

Printed and Published by J. Salmon Ltd., Sevenoaks, England ©

CHOCOLATE FUDGE CAKE

4 oz. hard margarine
10 oz. sugar
2 beaten eggs
6 oz. S.R. flour
2 oz. cocoa powder
2 drops vanilla essence
Pinch of salt
1 tablespoon milk

Grease two 9in. sandwich tins. Set oven to 350°F or Mark 4. Melt margarine gently in a pan. Put sugar in mixing bowl and add melted fat. Mix well. Beat in eggs, add sifted flour, cocoa and salt and 1 tablespoon milk. Add essence. Mix well together to give a stiff consistency. Line tins with greaseproof paper and pour mixture in. Smooth tops and cook for 20 minutes. Dust with icing sugar when cool and cut each round into convenient sized segments. These fudge slices are very popular with children. Serve the same day.

A FELL-SIDE FARM, CUMBERLAND

*U*PLANDS *B*ISCUITS

8 oz. hard margarine
5 oz. sugar
10 oz. S.R. flour
2 oz. custard powder
1 large egg
Pinch of salt

Grease baking trays. Set oven to 350°F or Mark 4. Beat fat and sugar until very soft. Add beaten egg and rest of ingredients. Knead well. Roll out and cut with plain biscuit cutter. Bake for 10 minutes until pale brown. When cold sandwich in pairs with home-made raspberry jam. Put a little white glacé icing on top and decorate with half a glacé cherry.

Ginger Shortcake

8 oz. butter
4 oz. caster sugar
10 oz. plain flour
2 teaspoons baking powder
2 teaspoons ground ginger

Icing
2 oz. butter
4 oz. icing sugar
1 teaspoon ground ginger
3 teaspoons syrup

Grease two 9in. sandwich tins. Set oven to 325°F or Mark 3. Beat butter and sugar until very soft. Sift in rest of ingredients and mix well. Divide into two and knead well with floured hands. Press down firmly into tins and bake for 40 minutes.

Icing – Melt syrup and butter in pan. Add sifted icing sugar and ginger. Pour over shortbread. Cut into wedges while warm.

DATE AND WALNUT SQUARES

4 oz. hard margarine
5 oz. caster sugar
4 oz. S.R. flour
1 egg
8 oz. chopped dates
4 oz. chopped walnuts
Plain chocolate to cover

Grease a Swiss Roll tin. Set oven to 350°F or Mark 4. Cream fat and sugar. Add egg, dates, walnuts and flour. If mixture is too stiff add 1 tablespoon of milk. Spread in tin. Bake for 30 minutes. When cool cover with plain melted chocolate and leave to set. Cut with sharp knife.

Luscious Lemon Cake

4 oz. soft margarine
6 oz. caster sugar
6 oz. S. R. flour
4 tablespoons milk
2 large eggs
Grated rind of 1 lemon

Syrup
3 rounded tablespoons icing sugar
3 tablespoons fresh lemon juice

Grease and line a 2lb. loaf tin. Set oven to 350°F or Mark 4. Cream fat and sugar, add eggs, sifted flour, finely grated lemon rind and milk. Mix well to a soft dropping consistency. Put in tin, smooth top and bake for 40–45 minutes until firm. Mix sifted icing sugar and lemon juice and pour over cake as soon as it comes out of the oven. Leave in tin until completely cold.

MARKET HOUSE, CHIPPING CAMPDEN, GLOUCESTERSHIRE

Picnic Slices

8 oz. plain or milk cooking
chocolate
2 oz. butter
4 oz. caster sugar
1 beaten egg
4 oz. dessicated coconut
2 oz. sultanas
2 oz. glacé cherries

Grease a Swiss Roll tin. Set oven to 300°F or Mark 2. Break chocolate into pieces and place in bowl over hot water. When melted, pour into bottom of Swiss Roll tin and leave to set. Cream fat and sugar, add egg, coconut, sultanas and chopped cherries. Mix well and spread evenly over chocolate. Bake for 30 minutes until golden brown. Leave to cool then cut into slices with a sharp knife.

GINGER DESSERT CAKE

6 oz. margarine
5 oz. soft brown sugar
3 eggs
6 oz. S.R. flour
3 rounded teaspoons
ground ginger

Filling
Whipped cream

Topping
Chocolate glacé icing

Grease and line two 8in. sandwich tins. Set oven to 350°F or Mark 4. Cream fat and sugar. Add eggs one at a time and beat well. Fold in flour and ginger. Divide into tins and bake for 25 minutes. When cool sandwich with sweetened whipped cream. Cover with chocolate icing made with 3 oz. plain chocolate, small knob of butter and 2 tablespoons water melted together. Add 8 oz. sifted icing sugar. Decorate with slices of crystallised ginger if liked – otherwise crystallised violet petals.

INTERIOR OF A SURREY COTTAGE

Rum and Currant Flan

8–9 oz. shortcrust pastry
2 oz. butter
4 oz. currants
4 oz. demerara sugar
1 teaspoon vanilla essence (optional)
3 teaspoons rum
1 small beaten egg

Set oven to 350°F or Mark 4. Roll out the pastry and line a 9in. diameter pie plate or flan dish. Melt the butter in a pan over gentle heat. Add the sugar and currants and stir. Remove from heat. Add essence and the rum. Add enough beaten egg to give the mixture a soft consistency. Pour into the uncooked pastry case and bake for about 20–25 minutes until risen and pastry is golden brown. Allow to cool and cover with a very thin layer of white glacé icing (if desired). Alternatively, roll out the left-over pastry, cut into strips and make a lattice pattern on top of flan before baking.

Fruit Loaf

1 lb. mixed dried fruit
6 oz. demerara sugar
1 teacup of strong tea
*Place above in a bowl and
leave overnight or as long
as possible*

1 oz. butter
8 oz. S.R. flour
1 egg
2 oz. walnuts
1 tablespoon caster sugar
Grated rind of 1 lemon and
1 orange

Grease and line a 2lb. loaf tin. Set oven to 325°F or Mark 3. Add flour, egg and grated rind to fruit mixture and beat well. Put in tin and level top. Scatter chopped walnuts on top then the tablespoon of caster sugar. Lastly dot with small pieces of the butter. Bake for $1-1\frac{1}{2}$ hours. Cool and wrap. Next day serve with butter.

Apricot Bread

14 oz. plain flour
1 oz. melted butter
1 egg
6 oz. sugar
$\frac{1}{2}$ teaspoon salt
1$\frac{1}{2}$ teaspoons baking powder
$\frac{1}{2}$ teaspoon bicarbonate of soda
3 oz. raisins *or* chopped walnuts
6 oz. dried apricots (cut small and soak in a little water)
Rind and juice of 1 orange - - made up to two-thirds of cup of liquid with more juice or quosh

Well grease 2lb. loaf tin. Set oven to 350°F or Mark 4. Sift dry ingredients into large bowl. Add raisins or nuts and apricots and mix well. Make a well in centre of mixture and add egg, butter and juice. Stir in. Place in tin and bake for 50–60 minutes. When cool wrap and keep for 24 hours before using. May be eaten plain or sliced with butter.

GINGER BISCUITS

8 oz. S.R. flour
4 oz. hard margarine
1 teaspoon bicarbonate of
soda
1 level teaspoon ground
ginger
4 oz. caster sugar
2 good tablespoons golden
syrup

Grease baking trays. Set oven to 375°F or Mark 5. Rub fat into flour, ground ginger and bicarbonate of soda. Add sugar and warmed syrup. Mix well to a stiff consistency. Roll into balls the size of a walnut with floured hands. Place on trays with room to spread and flatten with a fork. Bake for 10 minutes. Remove from trays while hot and place on cooling trays.

CROWCOMBE CROSS, SOMERSET

Almond Slices

Mix together
4 oz. caster sugar
4 oz. icing sugar
4 oz. ground almonds
2 oz. ground rice
1 whole egg
1 egg white
Apricot jam

Cover a Swiss Roll tin with shortcrust pastry.

Set oven to 375°F or Mark 5. Cover pastry with a layer of apricot jam. Then cover with the above mixture. Smooth over and top with sliced almonds or chopped walnuts. Bake for 20 minutes until pale brown. Slice and leave to cool.

 Toffee Bars

4 oz. butter
4 oz. brown sugar
1 egg yolk
2 oz. plain flour
2 oz. porridge oats

Topping
3 oz. plain chocolate
1 oz. butter
Chopped walnuts

Grease a Swiss Roll tin. Set oven to 375°F or Mark 5. Beat butter, sugar and egg yolk until smooth. Add flour and oats. Press mixture into tin and bake for 15–20 minutes. Cool slightly. Melt butter and chocolate and spread over mixture in the tin. Cover with chopped walnuts. Cut into bars while warm, but leave in tin until completely cold.

COTTAGE AT ROUTH, YORKSHIRE

Yorkshire Tea Cakes

2lb. strong plain flour
4 oz. lard
2 teaspoons salt
¾ pint lukewarm milk
1 egg
1 oz. fresh yeast
4 oz. sugar
4 oz. currants

Grease baking trays. Rub lard into flour and salt. Dissolve yeast and sugar in the lukewarm milk. Add to flour together with beaten egg. Knead to a soft dough (about 5–10 minutes). Fold in currants. Put in bowl. Cover with cloth and put in warm place until double in size. Knead gently. Divide and roll into 4in. rounds. Place on baking tray. Prick with fork. Leave for 30 minutes to rise, setting oven to 425°F or Mark 7. Bake 15–20 minutes. Cool on wire tray.

Rich Seed Cake

½lb. S.R. flour
½lb. sugar
½lb. butter
4 separated eggs
1 oz. carraway seeds
½ teaspoon nutmeg
½ teaspoon ground cinnamon

Grease and line a 7in. round cake tin. Set oven to 350°F or Mark 4. Cream butter and sugar. Add stiffly beaten egg whites, then add beaten yolks. Gradually add flour and spices. Put in tin and bake for 1 hour. This keeps well, and improves in flavour.

Sultana and Cherry Cake

¾lb. sultanas
¼lb. glacé cherries
4 oz. butter
4 oz. caster sugar
3 large eggs
A pinch of salt
6 oz. plain flour

Grease and line a 2lb. loaf tin. Set oven to 325°F or Mark 3. Cream fat and sugar. Add beaten eggs and flour gradually, leaving a little flour to mix in with the fruit and cherries. Bake for $1\frac{1}{2}$–$1\frac{3}{4}$ hours. Leave in tin to cool.

ORANGE AND ALMOND CAKE

2 oz. fine breadcrumbs
4 oz. ground almonds
Rind of 1 orange
Juice of 3 oranges
4 oz. caster sugar
2 eggs

Grease and line a 9in. tin. Set oven to 350°F or Mark 4. Combine breadcrumbs, almonds, rind and juice. Beat egg yolks and sugar. Stir into orange mixture. Then add stiffly beaten egg whites. Pour into tin. Bake for 30 minutes. This cake does not rise much. Leave to cool before turning out. Spread top with cream and decorate as you wish.

CASTLE COMBE, WILTSHIRE

Coconut Meringue Slices

3 oz. margarine
4 oz. sugar
2 egg yolks
2 tablespoons milk
6 oz. S.R. flour
½ teaspoon salt

Topping
2 stiffly beaten egg whites
2 oz. dessicated coconut
4 oz. sugar
1 oz. chopped nuts
1 oz. chopped glacé cherries

Grease a flat tin. Set oven to 350°F or Mark 4. Cream fat and sugar then add rest of ingredients. Press down firmly in tin. Mix ingredients for topping and place on top of mixture in tin. Bake for about 20 minutes until pale brown. Cut into slices.

Spicy Layer Cake

6 oz. plain flour
1 level teaspoon baking powder
$\frac{1}{2}$ level teaspoon salt
$\frac{1}{2}$ level teaspoon bicarbonate of soda
$\frac{1}{2}$ level teaspoon mixed spice
$\frac{1}{2}$ level teaspoon ground cinnamon
4 oz. margarine
5 oz. granulated sugar
3 oz. soft brown sugar
2 beaten eggs
1 small tin evaporated milk

Grease and line two 9in. sandwich tins. Set oven to 350°F or Mark 4. Sift all dry ingredients twice. Cream fat and sugars well. Add eggs, dry ingredients and milk. Divide between tins and bake for 30 minutes. Sandwich with lemon butter icing, and dredge top with icing sugar.

AN INN KITCHEN, KENT

Rich Almond Cake

4 oz. butter
5 oz. caster sugar
3 eggs
3 oz. ground almonds
1½ oz. plain flour
2 drops almond essence

Grease and line a 7in. deep cake tin. Set oven to 350°F or Mark 4. Soften butter and add sugar gradually, beating well. Add the eggs one at a time with one third of the almonds with each. Fold in the well-sieved flour and the essence. Bake for 40–45 minutes. When cool dust with caster sugar.

ℬUTTERMILK ℬREAD

1 lb. plain flour
1 level teaspoon cream of tartar
1 level teaspoon bicarbonate of soda
1 teaspoon salt
1 breakfast cup buttermilk (or use 1 dessertspoon vinegar made up to cupful with fresh milk)

Grease a flat tin. Set oven to 435°F or Mark 7. Sift flour and rest of dry ingredients into a bowl. Add just enough milk to make the dough adhere together in a ball. Divide dough into two, and shape into rounds. Place on greased tin. Mark the top of the bread with a knife and bake for 20 minutes. Eat the same day.

COCONUT CAKE

4 oz. margarine
2 drops almond essence
Rind of 1 lemon
3 oz. brown sugar
1 beaten egg
12 oz. plain flour
Apricot jam

Topping
1 beaten egg
3 oz. brown sugar
8 oz. coconut

Grease a Swiss Roll tin. Set oven to 350°F or Mark 4. Cream fat and sugar and essence, rind and egg. Add flour. Press into tin. Spread a layer of jam on top. Then cover with topping (mixed together). Bake for 20–30 minutes until firm. Cool before cutting and store in airtight tin.

GRASMERE GINGERBREAD

9 oz. brown wheatmeal
flour
3 oz. porridge oats
$\frac{3}{4}$ level teaspoon
bicarbonate of soda
$1\frac{1}{2}$ level teaspoons cream
of tartar
3 level teaspoons
ground ginger
9 oz. hard margarine
9 oz. soft brown sugar

Set oven to 325°F or Mark 3. Well grease a shallow tin 14in. by 9in. Put flour, oats, bicarbonate of soda, cream of tartar and ginger in a bowl. Add the margarine cut into small pieces. Rub in well with the fingertips until the mixture resembles breadcrumbs. Stir in the sugar. Put into tin and press down firmly with a floured fork. Bake for 20–30 minutes until pale brown. Cut into squares whilst warm and leave in tin until completely cold. Keeps well in an airtight tin.

NAB COTTAGE, RYDAL, WESTMORLAND

CARAMEL SHORTBREAD

4 oz. butter
6 oz. S.R. flour
2 oz. sugar

Topping
4 oz. caster sugar*
4 oz. butter*
2 tablespoons golden syrup*
1 small tin condensed milk*
Chocolate to cover*

*Place all these ingredients in a pan. Bring to boil for 5 minutes stirring continuously

Cream butter and sugar well and stir in flour and pinch of salt. Knead well and place in greased Swiss Roll tin. Bake at 325°F or Mark 3 for 30 minutes until pale brown.

Pour topping over cooked shortbread. When set cover with milk or plain chocolate. Cut into squares with sharp knife dipped in hot water.

ALMOND BISCUITS OR TUILES

3 oz. butter
3 oz. caster sugar
2 oz. plain flour
Pinch of salt
3 oz. shredded almonds

Grease baking trays. Set oven to 375°F or Mark 5. Soften butter. Add sugar and beat well. Sift flour and salt and add to mixture with the almonds. Put in teaspoonfuls on to trays, allowing plenty of room to spread. Bake for 6–8 minutes. Allow to cool for a few seconds then remove from tray with a sharp knife. Curl round a rolling pin until set. These are nice served with coffee, or fresh fruit salad.

THE GREEN, BROADWAY, WORCESTERSHIRE

BUTTER DROPS

4 oz. butter
4 oz. caster sugar
2 large beaten eggs
5 oz. plain flour
$\frac{1}{2}$ level teaspoon baking powder

Grease baking trays. Set oven to 325°F or Mark 3. Melt butter slowly in pan until it turns pale brown. Remove from heat and leave to cool for 10 minutes. Beat in sugar and eggs. Sift flour and baking powder and stir them in the pan. Place 5 teaspoonfuls of mixture on each tray – as they spread during cooking. Bake for about 20 minutes when they should be golden brown round the edges. Put on cooling trays straight away. Delicious with a cup of coffee.

Rice Loaf

4 oz. plain flour
1 level teaspoon baking
powder
Pinch of salt
4 oz. ground rice
2 oz. ground almonds
6 oz. butter
6 oz. caster sugar
3 eggs
1 tablespoon warm water

Grease and line a 2lb. loaf tin. Set oven to 350°F or Mark 4. Cream butter and sugar. Add eggs and dry ingredients gradually. Add warm water and stir until smooth. Turn into tin and bake about 1 hour until golden. A popular recipe for people who like a plain cake.

Banana Nut Bread

6 oz. sugar
4 oz. butter
2 eggs
3 tablespoons sour milk
1 teaspoon bicarbonate of soda
12 oz. S.R. flour
2 very ripe bananas
6 oz. chopped walnuts
Vanilla essence

Grease a 2lb. loaf tin. Set oven to 350°F or Mark 4. Cream butter and sugar, add well beaten eggs. Mash the bananas and add them with the flour, and soda mixed with the milk. Add one teaspoon vanilla essence and the nuts. Bake for 40–45 minutes until firm. When cold, slice and butter.

COFFEE CAKE

6 oz. soft margarine
6 oz. sugar
7 oz. S.R. flour
2 heaped teaspoons coffee powder
1 tablespoon hot water
Pinch of salt
Level teaspoon baking powder
3 beaten eggs

Grease and line two 9in. tins. Set oven to 375°F or Mark 5. Cream fat and sugar until soft. Dissolve the coffee powder in the hot water. Add beaten eggs, sifted flour, salt and baking powder. Add coffee mixture and mix well. Divide into tins and bake for 20 minutes. When cool decorate with coffee butter icing and chopped walnuts.

THE PLAGUE COTTAGES, EYAM, DERBYSHIRE

Coconut Cookies

2 egg whites
4 oz. caster sugar
6 oz. dessicated coconut
Rice paper

Grease baking sheet and cover with rice paper. Set oven to 325°F or Mark 3. Whisk egg whites very stiff. Fold in sugar and coconut. Drop spoonfuls on rice paper. Bake for 15 minutes. Cool before removing from tin.

DATE AND CHERRY CAKE

¾lb. sugar
¾lb S.R. flour
1 egg
½ teaspoon salt
½ teaspoon bicarbonate of soda
½ pint boiling water
4 oz. glacé cherries
4 oz. dates
2 oz. margarine
1 teaspoon vanilla essence

Grease and line a square tin. Set oven to 350°F or Mark 4. Rub fat into flour. Dissolve bicarbonate of soda in water. Chop cherries and dates to convenient size pieces. Add all dry ingredients, egg and liquid to flour and mix well. Bake for 1½ hours. When cold, slice and butter.

THE FORTIFIED END, OLD SOAR, KENT

Russian Tipsy Cake

1 oz. unsweetened chocolate
3 tablespoons water
3 eggs
$4\frac{1}{2}$ oz. caster sugar
$2\frac{1}{4}$ oz. plain flour
Pinch of salt
1 extra tablespoon plain flour

Filling
2 tablespoons fruit juice
2 tablespoons rum
$\frac{1}{2}$ pint double cream
Chocolate drops

Grease a 9in. tin then dust with caster sugar and flour. Set oven to 375°F or Mark 5. Melt chocolate in water. Whisk eggs and sugar in mixer at fast speed until thick. Fold in flour and salt. Divide into two parts. Add chocolate to one part and the extra flour to the other part. Put alternate spoonfuls in tin to give marbled effect. Bake for 30–40 minutes. When cool split it and spoon fruit juice and rum (mixed) over both parts. Fill middle with cream and decorate top with whirls of cream and chocolate drops.

FARMHOUSE SPONGE

3 large eggs separated
5 oz. caster sugar
4 oz. S.R. flour
Pinch of salt

Grease and flour two 9in. sandwich tins. Set oven to 375°F or Mark 5. Warm surface of bowl in oven. Whisk egg whites until stiff – add sugar and yolks and whisk until thick and creamy. Fold in flour and salt with metal spoon. Divide into tins and put straight into heated oven. Bake for 20–30 minutes. When cold sandwich with jam and whipped cream.